INDUSTRIAL AGE
MEDICINE

Rebecca Vickers

www.raintreepublishers.co.uk
Visit our website to find out more information about Raintree books.

To order:
☎ Phone 0845 6044371
🖹 Fax +44 (0) 1865 312263
🖳 Email myorders@raintreepublishers.co.uk

Customers from outside the UK please telephone +44 1865 312262

Raintree is an imprint of Capstone Global Library Limited, a company incorporated in England and Wales having its registered office at 7 Pilgrim Street, London, EC4V 6LB – Registered company number: 6695582

Edited by Andrew Farrow, Adam Miller, and
  Vaarunika Dharmapala
Designed by Philippa Jenkins
Picture research by Ruth Blair
Originated by Capstone Global Library Ltd
Printed and bound in China by Leo Paper
  Products Ltd

ISBN 978 1 406 23873 0 (hardback)
16 15 14 13 12
10 9 8 7 6 5 4 3 2 1

British Library Cataloguing in Publication Data
Vickers, Rebecca.
Industrial age medicine. -- (Medicine through the ages)
610.9'033-dc22
A full catalogue record for this book is available from the British Library.

Acknowledgements
We would like to thank the following for permission to reproduce photographs: Alamy pp. 6 (© North Wind Picture Archives), 12, 24, 29 (© The Protected Art Archive), 32 (© Paris Pierce), 33 (© Vario Images GmbH & Co. KG), 39 (© Photo Researchers); Corbis pp. 10 (© The Gallery Collection), 23 (© Bettmann); Courtesy of NLM p. 28; Getty Images pp. 18, 26, 27, 35 (Hulton Archive), 21 (Buyenlarge), 22 (MPI), 30 (SSPL), 36 (Museum of the City of New York); Mary Evans Picture Library p. 14; Science Photo Library pp. 19 (Jim Varney), 20, 38 (National Library of Medicine), Wellcome Library, London pp. 4, 5, 8, 9, 11, 16, 19, 25, 31, 34, 37, 41.

Cover photograph of a painting of Florence Nightingale attending a patient at Scutari Barracks, Turkey, reproduced with permission of Alamy (© Mary Evans Picture Library).

Every effort has been made to contact copyright holders of any material reproduced in this book. Any omissions will be rectified in subsequent printings if notice is given to the publisher.

Contents

Some words are shown in bold, **like this**. You can find out what they mean by looking in the glossary. You can also look out for them in the "Word Station" box at the bottom of each page.

Medicine on the move

By the mid-18th century, the profession of medicine was entering a period of rapid change and development. Many old ideas about the human body and how to cure and prevent diseases were being questioned. Doctors themselves were becoming better trained and more professional and organized in their approach.

This etching by William Hogarth is known as both *The Company of Undertakers* and *A Consultation of Physicians* (1736). It shows that doctors were traditionally viewed very negatively. They were seen as overpaid and lazy, and some were regarded as **quacks** who sold useless remedies. This view began to change in the mid-18th century as the profession became more regulated.

Becoming a doctor

One of the routes a young man could follow to become a doctor was to attend university. Universities in Edinburgh, London, Leiden in the Netherlands, and Salerno in Italy, were all respected for the medical training they offered. Other young men **apprenticed** themselves to a medical professional, while still others paid to attend private medical lectures. There were no set medical curriculums, no specific requirements, and only a few professional organizations.

WORD STATION
quack unqualified person who claims to have medical knowledge

Sticking to what they knew

Most of the equipment used by doctors had not changed very much in the previous 200 years. The methods used to **diagnose** patients were usually not scientific. The microscope (1590s) and the thermometer (1709) had both been invented, but doctors still preferred to poke and prod their patients and examine their urine. However, even if doctors *had* wanted to use the thermometer, until the mid-19th century this instrument was often about 30 centimetres (1 foot) long and took half an hour to register a temperature. The most advanced medical knowledge was in the field of **anatomy**. Most doctors attended **dissecting** rooms as part of their training.

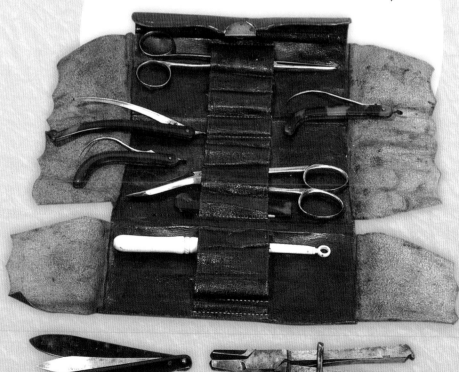

Although some new instruments were available to doctors by 1750, most doctors could fit the equipment and treatments available to them into a leather roll like this one.

COMMON CONFUSIONS

Why dissect bodies?

From medieval times, medical schools had trained doctors to understand the inner workings of the human body and its structure by dissecting dead bodies. This meant that when surgeons dealt with living patients, they knew what they were looking for and could be quick. With no way to drug patients to deal with pain, speed was very important!

Rapid changes

From the mid-18th century, there were many rapid changes in medical understanding, training, procedures, and equipment. Why were the conditions at this time so perfect for such a transformation?

The process we now call the Industrial Revolution – when the economy of a country begins to change from small-scale local production of goods to large-scale factory production – started during the second half of the 18th century. People moved from the country to work in the growing industries based in cities. The crowded and unsanitary living conditions led to the spread of diseases and air and water pollution.

LIVERPOOL

In 1750, the city of Liverpool had a population of 22,000 people. As a major port and industrial centre, it changed and grew rapidly during the Industrial Revolution. By 1900, its population had expanded to 450,000 people.

The Industrial Revolution led to **urbanization** and crowded towns. These conditions were the perfect breeding grounds for **contagious** diseases.

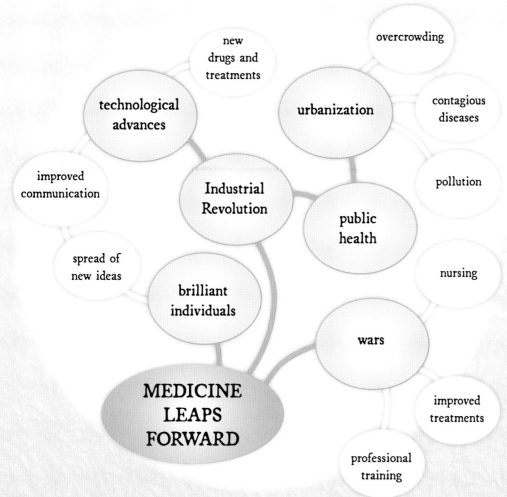

- new drugs and treatments
- overcrowding
- technological advances
- urbanization
- contagious diseases
- improved communication
- Industrial Revolution
- pollution
- public health
- spread of new ideas
- nursing
- brilliant individuals
- wars
- MEDICINE LEAPS FORWARD
- improved treatments
- professional training

This diagram shows the many factors that led to advances in medical science.

HERMAN BOERHAAVE
(1668–1738)

Herman Boerhaave was the first modern medical educator. He set the standards for **clinical** teaching and created the teaching hospital. As well as being a doctor, Boerhaave was a botanist and head of the chemistry department at Leiden University.

Did you know?
The famous British dictionary writer, Dr Samuel Johnson, published a biography of Herman Boerhaave in 1739, four months after Boerhaave's death.

Science and technology

Some of the technologies that came into use during the Industrial Revolution could be applied to scientific work as well as business. For example, better technology led to improvements in glass-making, and this in turn made it possible to build microscopes with better lenses.

The medical profession was starting to see the advantages of learning about other sciences as well as learning from each other. Doctors such as Herman Boerhaave, Professor of Medicine at Leiden University in the Netherlands, saw the importance of record keeping and using new scientific discoveries. These ideas spread as students and staff moved between medical schools.

The work of brilliant and innovative individuals also had a huge impact on medical progress. Some, such as Louis Pasteur (see pages 16–17) and Robert Koch (see page 18), made discoveries and proved theories that would eventually change medicine forever.

Beginning to understand diseases

The most important change in medical practice was an increased understanding of what caused illness and disease. For thousands of years, the medical profession had believed that diseases were spread by invisible **contamination** that moved through the air. These clouds of death were known as *miasma*, an ancient Greek word meaning pollution or stain.

This is a state-of-the art microscope from the mid-18th century.

WORD STATION
miasma unpleasant or unhealthy substance in the air

Seeing the causes of disease

The improved microscope lenses of the mid-18th century meant that scientists could now see much smaller things. Some thought that very small living things, usually referred to as "animalcules", might have something to do with the spread of illnesses. John Pringle conducted research into **epidemics** in prisons, hospitals, and military camps. He recognized that the close confinement of large numbers of people resulted in a rapid spread of infections.

Could this be something to do with animalcules? Pringle had seen these through microscopes and he had read about them in the works of the Dutch scientist Anton van Leeuwenhoek. Pringle thought that these living agents could be the cause of the **dysentery** and typhus fevers he was keen to prevent. However, he could not see beyond miasma theory, and still thought that it was the air that had became rotten and infected.

JOHN PRINGLE
(1707-1782)

Pringle was a Scottish doctor and researcher. He worked tirelessly to stop the massive numbers of deaths that seemed to occur whenever large groups of people were housed closely together. His obsession with finding ways to prevent diseases spreading led him to research **antiseptic** substances for the cleaning of surfaces, individuals, and their clothing.

Did you know?
John Pringle was the first to use the word *antiseptic* to mean something that works against and destroys anything septic (infected and rotten).

Inoculation

The most feared of all major diseases at the time was **smallpox**. This disease killed most of the people who caught it, and those who did not die were often left blind and hideously scarred, particularly on the face. Some people tried to protect themselves with the risky method of **inoculation**. This involved being deliberately infected with pus taken from the smallpox sores of someone suffering a mild form of the disease.

MARY WORTLEY MONTAGU
(1689–1762)

Mary Montagu was an English aristocrat and wife of the ambassador to Turkey. While she was in Turkey, she witnessed smallpox inoculations. On her return, she introduced the method to England. Soon people could pay to be inoculated. A piece of thread was soaked in pus taken from a smallpox **lesion**. It was then introduced into a cut in the arm of the patient. The patient would be isolated in a warm room until they had gone through a mild form of the disease. If the patient survived, they would be unlikely to catch smallpox again. However, there was always a risk that the smallpox inoculation would develop into a life-threatening form of the disease.

Did you know?
Montagu's letters home are a good source of information about life in the Ottoman Empire, which included Turkey, and was one of the largest and most long-lasting empires in history.

WORD STATION
smallpox disease characterized by pus-filled blisters

This early 19th-century cartoon shows Edward Jenner vaccinating some worried patients. They are sprouting cow heads – a reference to Jenner's experiments with cowpox vaccine.

Edward Jenner's cowpox experiments

English doctor Edward Jenner (1749–1823) believed that people who caught cowpox, a mild form of smallpox, never went on to get the deadlier version of the disease. Jenner noticed this effect in milkmaids who had regular contact with cows. In 1796, he used a healthy eight-year-old boy, James Phipps, to test his **hypothesis**.

Jenner collected pus from a cowpox scab on a milkmaid and put it in a cut on James's arm. James became a bit ill but recovered in a few days. Then Jenner infected James with smallpox in the same way. Nothing happened! James's **vaccination** with cowpox *did* protect him from smallpox. Within a very short period of time, vaccination against smallpox spread around the world.

Cleaning up medicine

By using observation, **hypothesis**, and experimentation, Edward Jenner gave the medical world a tool in the fight against the dreadful disease **smallpox**. At the same time, other doctors were hitting upon more ways to keep diseases from spreading.

These soldiers from the American Civil War (1861–1865) are dressing wounds in a makeshift hospital tent. Conditions such as this were dirty and dangerous.

John Pringle and others had noticed that diseases spread very quickly in crowded conditions. Diseases such as "jail fever" and "hospital fever" were rapidly transmitted between people, resulting in very high **mortality** rates.

However, doctors could only experiment with what *seemed* to work. They did not know why one experiment was successful and another a failure. This was because they did not know about **microbes**, by which most diseases are spread from one person to another.

Jail fever travels to the courts

Pringle recognized that typhus fevers were not only causing **epidemics** in jails. They also were travelling with inmates when they went to court! There were a number of cases of court attendees, including judges, contracting jail fever. Pringle introduced a set of measures that included washing inmates before they went to court and giving them new, clean clothes to wear. His reforms worked when they were put into practice, but he met with resistance to many of his calls for change.

Pringle's *Observations*

In 1744, Pringle was made Physician General to the British Army. In 1752, the first edition of his *Observations on the Diseases of the Army* was published. This volume was significant for putting into print the importance that Pringle placed on cross-infection between people and their belongings as a way in which diseases were spread.

This table shows how many years the average person could expect to live in these countries in 1800. What factors do you think account for the differences between nations?

Life expectancy at birth in 1800	
United Kingdom	40
United States	39
Germany	38
Australia	35
France	32
India	25

Germs: small, but deadly

Many doctors and other scientists had seen living "animalcules" through microscopes or in drawings. Some, such as US doctor John Crawford (1746–1813), thought these sources of transmission were members of the insect kingdom, with a similar life cycle: "Man has invisible, insect-like enemies, numerous and incapable of detection by the ordinary senses." However, there was a very strong resistance to the idea that these living things were causing and spreading diseases.

RIGHT IDEA, WRONG TIME

John Crawford suffered for promoting an idea ahead of its time. In an 1813 letter to another well-known US doctor, Benjamin Rush, Crawford complained about his growing debts, saying he had lost all his business by "propagating [promoting] an unpopular opinion in medicine, namely that all diseases were occasioned [caused] by *animalculae*".

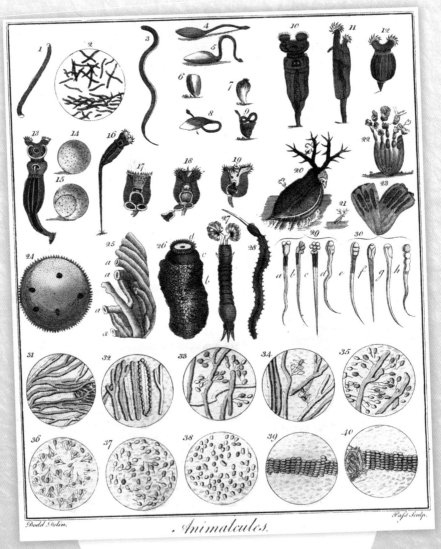

Animalcules.

These were some of the animalcules identified by scientists by 1794.

Ignaz Semmelweis

In 1844, Hungarian doctor Ignaz Semmelweis (1818–1865) began working at a hospital in Vienna, Austria. The hospital had two public maternity clinics. Semmelweis soon noticed that many more women were dying after childbirth in one of the clinics than in the other. One clinic was staffed by doctors from the hospital and the other by midwives. Semmelweis was horrified when his **statistical** analysis of the deaths showed that it was the doctors who were making one of the clinics into a death trap.

While the midwives only delivered babies, the doctors also performed **post-mortems** and **dissected** the bodies of women who had died during or after childbirth. They did not wash their hands or change their clothing between duties. Semmelweis did not understand how this was causing the spread of infection, but he decided to find ways to stop it. When he got the doctors to wash their hands in chloride of lime before touching living patients, the death rate fell rapidly. The washing was killing the germs that caused infections. However, Semmelweis's methods were not approved of and he lost his job in 1849.

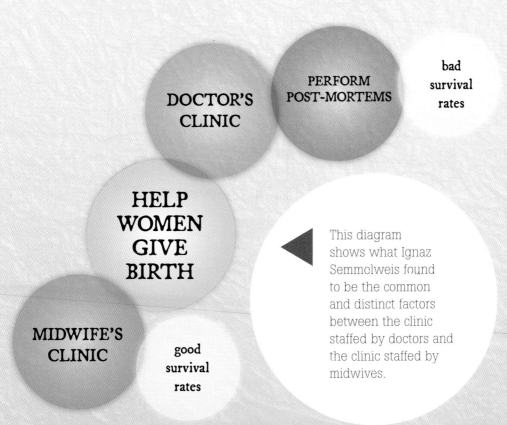

This diagram shows what Ignaz Semmelweis found to be the common and distinct factors between the clinic staffed by doctors and the clinic staffed by midwives.

The proof of germ theory

By the 19th century, improved microscopes meant that many people had seen animalcules. However, most doctors and scientists believed that these **microbes** were created by diseases, not that they were the agents that *caused* diseases. This theory was called spontaneous generation. Then a French scientist, Louis Pasteur (1822–1895), proved them wrong.

This 1885 drawing shows Louis Pasteur using a microscope in his laboratory.

WORD STATION
microbe very tiny living thing that can carry disease

Proving the link

Pasteur was researching the reasons why alcohol would sometimes go sour during the **fermentation** process. When he examined the liquid under a microscope, he could see living microbes. His **hypothesis** was that the germs were getting into the open vats of liquid through the air and **contaminating** it.

Pasteur put water into a special curved, "swan-neck" flask, then heated it to boiling. The boiling killed off any germs in the water, and the rising warm air was pushed out around the bend in the neck of the flask, taking any germs with it. No germs "spontaneously generated" in this water.

However, when the neck of the flask was broken and the previously **sterile** water left open to the air, it once again became contaminated with germs.

Matching germs to diseases

This successful experiment proved a connection between specific germs and the contamination of the liquid. Armed with this knowledge, Pasteur very quickly went on to do several very important things:

- He developed methods to destroy and prevent contamination and infection. The most famous is pasteurization, where heating a liquid at specific temperatures for set lengths of time destroys germs, keeping it safe and fresh.

- He started to work on specific diseases, mostly those that affected animals, developing vaccines and other treatments. A major success was finding the germ that caused **rabies**, as well as a treatment for the disease.

- He convinced many doctors, particularly surgeons, that they should **sterilize** their equipment and instruments. This killed many of the germs that would have been transferred from patient to patient.

COMMON CONFUSIONS

What are germs?

Using the word *germ* makes it sound as if there is just one type of thing that causes all diseases. In fact, there are many different types of microbes, including bacteria, viruses, and fungi that cause contamination, infection, and specific diseases.

Seeking the microbes

Pasteur said the next step was to work out which germ caused which disease – to "seek the microbe". Only then could treatments and preventions be developed. In 1872, the German doctor Robert Koch (1843–1910) started to do just that. Koch used his skills as a doctor as well as experimental methods. He used new technology, such as dyes to colour microscopic slides, and cameras to photograph his results. In this way, Koch identified anthrax (1876), septicaemia (1878), tuberculosis (1882), and cholera (1883). The work of Koch and others made it possible to create vaccines and other treatments for some of the most deadly diseases.

A NEW SCIENCE

Robert Koch is often referred to as the father of the science of microbiology (the study of tiny living things). Bacteria were first identified by Dutch microscope maker, Anton van Leeuwenhoek in 1676, but Koch's new methods made the examination of very small living things into an organized science. His use of dyes to stain samples and culture mediums to grow bacteria made identification much easier. Today, microbiologists study all aspects of bacteria, viruses, fungi, and algae.

Robert Koch started his medical career as a doctor in the Prussian army.

Joseph Lister

Joseph Lister (1827–1912) was a young professor of surgery at the University of Glasgow when he became familiar with Pasteur's work in the mid-1860s. He realized that as well as contaminating the brewing process, germs were also the cause of the infections which killed so many patients after surgery. How could he make an operating theatre a germ-free environment?

Joseph Lister used a disinfectant called carbolic acid in operating theatres such as this one. The disinfectant was sprayed from the pump on the right.

Lister knew he would have to find some way to kill germs. He started to experiment with carbolic acid, a disinfectant used to combat the odour of rotting sewage. Very quickly he realized he had hit upon something that worked. Soaking surgical bandages in carbolic acid meant that wounds were protected from infection. When all other aspects of operating theatres were sprayed with carbolic acid, including the surgeons and the patients, the death rates fell dramatically.

Today, disinfectants are still used to keep germs out of hospital wards.

COMMON CONFUSIONS

More surgery, more death

When **anaesthetics** became widely used at the end of the 1840s (see pages 22–23), doctors started performing more operations. They could also take more time as they did not have to worry about the pain patients were suffering. However, this also meant that the theatres and instruments were being used for more people and the germs had more time to enter open wounds. Pain management had improved, but hygiene had not. In the 20 years after anaesthetics were introduced, the death rate went up, not down. This is called the "Black Period" of surgery.

Hospitals

In the early 19th century, hospitals were mostly for the sick poor, as other people were usually treated at home. Hospitals were dirty and crowded and they provided very little in the way of useful medical treatments. However, during the next 100 years, hospitals changed out of all recognition.

What changed?

Three main developments during the 19th century changed hospitals:

- *Science changed.* Even before the gradual acceptance of germ theory in the 1870s and 1880s (see pages 16–19), John Pringle, Florence Nightingale (see pages 30–31), and Ignaz Semmelweis, among others, had stressed the need for cleanliness and order. The development of pain control methods such as **anaesthetics** (see pages 22–23) meant that surgery could be more complex and take longer. The introduction of effective **antiseptics** from the late 1860s decreased deaths from the diseases and infections patients contracted in hospital. Hospitals really were safer.

As shown in this illustration from 1807, until the 1850s, nurses were often untrained and incompetent. Nursing was not considered a profession, and many nurses were glorified babysitters of the sick and dying.

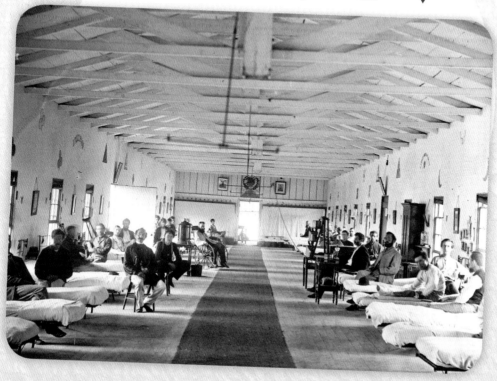

By the time this military hospital in Washington DC was operating in 1865, hospitals were safer, better equipped, and staffed by medical professionals.

- *Technology developed.* Laboratory testing of samples, specialist clinics, and eventually very large machinery such as X-ray machines meant that hospitals offered services not available elsewhere.

- *Training of medical professionals became more **systematic**.* During the 19th century, the medical profession started to organize itself. Teaching hospitals became the norm. Lectures, ward rounds, and research in hospitals formed part of every doctor's professional development. Medical bodies, such as the British Medical Association, started setting standards and membership requirements. The first British school for nurse training, the Institution of Nursing Sisters, was founded by Elizabeth Fry in 1840. This was followed by other nursing schools, in particular the Nightingale School of Nursing at St Thomas's Hospital in London in 1860. Remarkably, while in 1840 there were no trained nurses in Britain, by 1900, there were 64,000!

ELIZABETH FRY
(1780–1845)

Elizabeth Fry was born into a Quaker family in Norwich, and from a young age she was involved in **philanthropic** activities. She promoted **smallpox vaccination** and worked tirelessly for prison improvements, particularly for women's prisons. After visiting a training school for nurses in Germany in 1840, she returned and founded the Institution for Nursing Sisters.

Did you know?
Fry was **dyslexic**, and overcame her educational problems to focus on helping others.

Preventing pain

Operations done without anaesthetics had to be performed quickly with only the aid of **opiates** and alcohol to lessen the pain. The pain itself could be unbearable to the patient, and the shock of the pain could also prove fatal.

In the mid-1840s, Horace Wells, a dentist working in Connecticut, USA, wanted to make his patients more comfortable during dental treatments. He started experimenting with inhaled nitrous oxide gas to make his patients woozy or unconscious. He had mixed success. Another dentist, William Morton, working in Boston, USA, had better luck with another gas, called ether. In October 1846, he gave ether to a patient while a surgeon removed a tumour from the patient's neck. This public operation was a painless success. Within two months, ether was also being used in Britain.

A NEW NAME

The word *anaesthetic* is derived from a Greek word for "insensibility". It was given to the new method of pain relief by American doctor Oliver Wendell Homes, Sr in 1846.

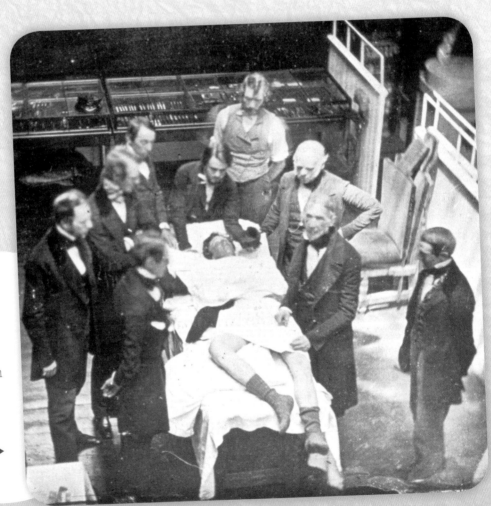

Ether is being used on this patient during an operation in Boston, USA, in 1846.

WORD STATION
opiate drug containing opium or made from opium

 Chloroform got a boost in popularity when Queen Victoria (seated) used it in 1853 for pain relief during the birth of her eighth child, Leopold. She referred to the effects of the chloroform as "soothing, quieting, and delightful beyond measure".

ROBERT LISTON
(1794–1847)

The famous Scottish surgeon Robert Liston was the first in Britain to use ether during major surgery. On 21 December 1846, he amputated the leg of Frederick Churchill using ether as an anaesthetic. The patient felt no pain, and Liston was converted to the use of anaesthetics.

Did you know?
Liston was legendary for the speed of his surgery, usually amputating limbs in under a minute!

WHAT WAS WRONG WITH ETHER?

James Simpson disliked ether for several reasons:
- It was a highly flammable gas.
- It irritated some patients' lungs, causing them to cough during surgery.
- It had a very strong and unpleasant smell.

Chloroform is better

James Young Simpson (1811–1870) was the professor of Midwifery at Edinburgh University when he decided that there must be a substance that would relieve pain like ether, but did not have its bad points. His experiments, including testing on himself and his colleagues, led him in late 1847 to chloroform. It was stronger and faster acting than ether, and easier to give to patients. Although there were those who disapproved of making a patient unconscious to prevent pain, it gradually gained support. Chloroform was the most common anaesthetic used until 1900. Ether then came back into favour when it was shown that chloroform use could permanently damage the liver and cause heart attacks and breathing difficulties.

The growth of public health

The Industrial Revolution, which began in the second half of the 18th century, led to **urbanization**, population growth, poverty, and pollution. As the major cities grew, the living conditions of the urban poor worsened. The British government did nothing to provide better water supplies or remove rubbish and sewage. Typhoid fever, tuberculosis, and influenza were commonplace. Then, cholera arrived.

Government jumps in

By the end of the first great cholera **epidemic** in Britain in 1832, over 20,000 people had died. The government eventually tried to combat this horrific disease. Regulations were enforced requiring immediate burial of cholera victims, and local Boards of Health were set up to try to find methods of dealing with it. Since the disease was still presumed to spread through a **miasma**, barrels of tar were burnt in city streets in attempts to "purify" the air. However, nothing worked. Death by cholera occurred so fast it was commonly said that people could be well at breakfast and dead by dinner.

These crowded homes on the Lower East Side of New York City were a breeding ground for disease and death (see pages 28–29).

In this drawing from 1849, the clothes of cholera victims are being burnt and thrown in the river in Exeter. Drinking water for the city came from the river. In 1832, no one knew that cholera was transmitted through water.

In the years after the 1832 epidemic, various reports, some ordered by the government, confirmed that most of the urban poor lived in squalid, unhealthy conditions. Pressure was growing for what became known as "sanitary reform" – cleaning up towns by improving water supplies, sewage, rubbish collection, and living conditions. Many politicians opposed the government getting involved in people's lives in this way, and were against passing a Public Health Bill.

Not again!

Then, after over 15 years without a great epidemic, cholera struck Britain again in 1848. The Public Health Bill was finally approved. The Public Health Act set up voluntary Boards of Health all over the country. If there was support, then a local Board could set about improving the water and sewage systems.

John Snow works it out

The next big cholera outbreak in London struck in 1854. Most doctors and politicians still believed that cholera was transmitted in bad, smelly air. However, London doctor John Snow had written an article in 1849 suggesting that cholera entered the body through the mouth. When the new outbreak started, Snow plotted every case that occurred on a map to try to show where the disease originated. He traced the disease to a public water pump. When he ordered the pump handle removed, the number of cases of cholera fell. Cholera *was* spread through the water and into victims' mouths, not through the air!

EDWIN CHADWICK
(1800–1890)

Edwin Chadwick was a British social reformer. He collected information about the living conditions of the urban poor, particularly in the East End of London. His report shocked the country. Chadwick was convinced that if it were possible to make cities cleaner, then the urban population would be healthier, would be able to work harder, and would cost the government less money in poor relief payments.

Did you know?
Chadwick was a firm believer in the miasma theory. He thought if London got rid of its foul smell, everyone's health would improve.

The Great Stink of 1858

Once John Snow had confirmed that cholera was carried in water, it became even more important that something was done to make the water safer in London. It was the biggest city in the world, with a population of over 2.75 million. However, nothing had been done to sort out the water and sewage mess.

The massive engineering project that gave London a functioning sewer system was planned and built under the control of Joseph Bazalgette (1819–1891), standing top right. When he died, an obituary claimed that he had added 20 years to the lifespan of every Londoner.

By the summer of 1858, the Thames had virtually become a river of human and animal waste. Waterborne diseases, such as cholera and typhoid, were common. The smell had become overwhelmingly horrible, and became known as the "Great Stink" of 1858. Suddenly, the misguided fear of cholera from the miasma of smell in the city gave the authorities the push they needed. London would finally get the sewer system it so desperately needed. The last bad outbreak of cholera in London was in 1866. By 1868, after 10 years, the sewers and water supply systems were finished.

What is a tenement?

The word *tenement* often makes everyone think of crowded, poverty-stricken urban slums, but it originally meant any rented building. In 1867, New York state law gave "tenement" a specific legal definition: a building lived in independently by three or more families or by more than two families on a floor.

New York City

London was not the only city in the 19th century where overcrowding and filthy conditions were killing its residents. New York City in the United States expanded from 60,000 citizens in 1800 to over 3.5 million by 1900, as wave after wave of immigrants swelled its population. As its population grew, so did its public health problems.

Epidemics of yellow fever struck the city in 1795, 1799, and 1803, killing many. In 1805, the authorities set up a Board of Health to examine how the city could protect itself. Unfortunately, over the next 50 years, the Board only reacted if something terrible happened, such as an epidemic. By 1850, the average life expectancy for a New Yorker was only 20 years, 8 months!

This cartoon from the time makes fun of the first New York Board of Health. It only reacted when disaster struck and did not plan for the future.

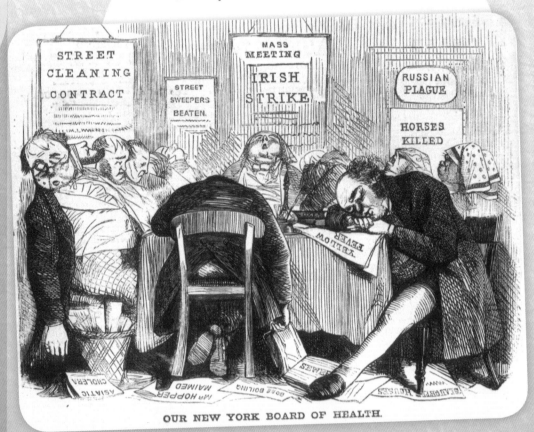

OUR NEW YORK BOARD OF HEALTH.

Tenement dwellers, such as these children, lived in a combination of poverty, filth, and overcrowding. They also faced corrupt landlords and government officials. Many children in the tenements died from **malnutrition**.

The 1866 Metropolitan Bill of Health

From 1859 to 1866, social reformers had pushed for an independent body to sort out New York City's disastrous public health situation. In 1866, the Metropolitan Bill of Health gave power to a commission appointed by the state governor with some doctors as members, but this was only temporary. By 1870, the **corrupt** mayor of the city was back in charge.

Public pressure for change meant that improvements did start to happen, at least in the control of diseases and provision of clean water. By the end of the century, the tenement slums were still present, but a **systematic** approach was being taken to prevent and control diseases and to inspect food, including water and milk, to make sure it was healthy and fit to eat.

War and changes in medicine

During the 19th century, three major wars had an impact on changes that took place in medicine: the Crimean War, the American Civil War, and the Franco-Prussian War.

The Crimean War (1853–1856)

The Crimean War was fought between the Russian Empire on one side and an alliance including the British and French on the other. The war is often remembered for the story of Florence Nightingale.

In 1854, Nightingale, accompanied by 38 nurses, went to the Turkish port of Scutari, where sick and wounded British soldiers were treated. Nightingale's aim was to improve the recovery rates of the wounded soldiers. She found the conditions there dirty and overcrowded, with inadequate medical supplies and uncooperative staff.

Out on the battlefields of the mid–19th century, a surgeon often had to amputate mangled limbs with saws like these.

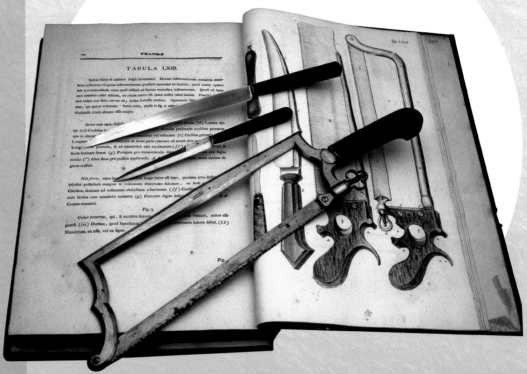

By 1856, Nightingale had put in place new measures and methods of treatment. Hygiene was greatly improved and conditions were less crowded. As a result, the death rate fell from 42 per cent to only 2 per cent. However, it was after Nightingale returned to England that she had the most impact.

- She used money from a public fund set up in her name to develop and set standards for the training of nurses.

- She wrote the book that became the training manual for the profession, *Notes on Nursing* (1859).

- She gave evidence to the government and wrote many recommendations as to how the army medical services should be improved and organized, and how soldiers should be treated.

- She championed the cause of "sanitary reform", meaning the importance of hygiene and improving living conditions in order to promote health and prevent disease.

Florence Nightingale became famous as the "lady with the lamp" in Scutari. She would often wander the wards at night to make sure the patients were being well looked after.

COMMON CONFUSIONS

Was Scutari a triumph for Nightingale?

In 1857, Florence Nightingale examined **statistical** information about deaths in the Crimea. She realized many deaths during 1854–1855 had been caused by hospital conditions and not by battlefield injuries and **malnutrition**.

Although she made sure that men were treated for injuries, **deloused**, and given clean clothes and blankets, it was overcrowding, bad sanitation, and lack of ventilation that spread fevers and infections. In an 1857 letter, she said of the hospital, "disease was chiefly generated within the building itself". Total British losses in the Crimea were 16,000 from sickness, 2,600 battlefield deaths, and 1,800 wounded.

The American Civil War (1861–1865)

The huge numbers of men involved in the American Civil War created new problems and challenges for those whose task it was to treat the injured. Organizational and **logistical** changes were made by the Union army during the war that are still part of the way medical services are run in modern armed forces. Most of these changes and innovations were the work of one man, Jonathan Letterman (1824–1872). Starting the war as a surgeon, by June 1862 he was the Medical Director of the entire Union army. He introduced:

- an ambulance corps with trained stretcher bearers and wagon drivers to move the wounded away from the action

- three different treatment stations – a first aid treatment area on the battlefield, small battlefield hospitals near the fighting for emergency surgery and other required treatment, and large hospitals away from the fighting for long-term treatment, recovery, and rehabilitation

- the concept of **triage**, where the wounded are categorized with attention given first to those most likely to survive.

During the American Civil War, organized transport for the injured was provided by the Army of the Potomac's ambulance corps.

WORD STATION
logistical relating to the provision of facilities, movement of people, and obtaining of supplies

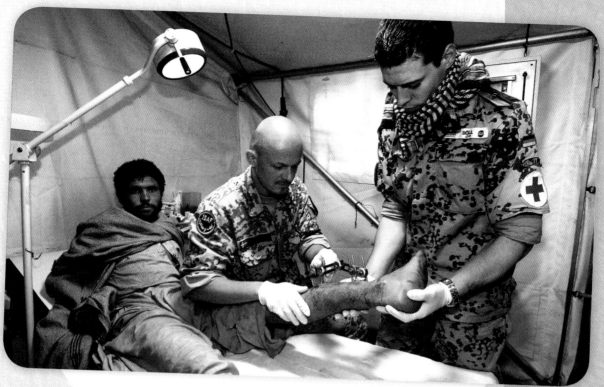

Just as in the past, modern war zones, such as Afghanistan, require medical staff to work in difficult conditions.

The Franco-Prussian War (1870–1871)

The Franco-Prussian War was a short conflict between France and the German states which France eventually lost, and which led to the unification of Germany. The countries remained rivals after the conflict had ended.

At this time, each country had a famous medical scientific researcher: Louis Pasteur in France and Robert Koch in Germany. Each new discovery made by one of these men added to the national prestige of his country. The money and support that each man received from his country was good for the future of medicine, but was the result of continuing national tension and rivalry.

Each man was given enough money to support a research team, and research institutes for them to work in were founded in each country, the Institute Pasteur in France (1887) and the Institute for Infectious Diseases in Germany (1891).

NEUTRAL MEDICINE

Before the end of the 18th century, John Pringle got warring sides to agree to the neutrality of battlefield hospitals and their staff. This continues today, particularly through the work of the Red Cross, the Red Crescent, and other medical charities in war zones.

Women and medicine

By the mid-19th century, many jobs were still considered unsuitable for women. Teaching, being a companion, or being a governess was all that a woman could realistically hope for. However, things were beginning to change.

Making nursing a proper job

When Florence Nightingale told her parents that she wished to train as a nurse, they were horrified. She said, "It was as if I wanted to be a kitchen maid." They thought of nurses as either nuns or the old, lazy, drunken women portrayed by authors of the time. In 1856, Florence Nightingale set up her first nursing training school at St Thomas's Hospital in London.

Before Florence Nightingale (seated at the centre in a shawl), these young women would not have had a chance to become members of a respected profession.

LINDA RICHARDS
(1841–1930)

Linda Richards was the first American woman to professionally train as a nurse. Having nursed her own mother and her fiancé on their deathbeds, she joined the first group of five women to attend nurse training at the New England Hospital for Women and Children in Boston. After qualifying in 1873, she worked for a year and then dedicated the rest of her working life to the promotion and establishment of quality nurse training colleges across the United States.

Soon schools of nursing sprung up at hospitals all over the United Kingdom. This proved that Florence Nightingale had identified a real need, and nursing soon became a socially acceptable profession for respectable women.

Women dentists

The 19th century also saw the acceptance of women into training courses that allowed them to become fully qualified dentists. Some women had **apprenticed** themselves to dentists and learned on the job. Then, in 1865, an American woman, Lucy Hobbs Taylor (1833–1910), entered the Ohio College of Dental Surgery. Taylor had trained as a dentist through private study and had practised dentistry in the states of Ohio and Iowa. After the Iowa State Dental Society allowed her to join, this official acceptance helped her return to formal training. Although the first British woman dentist did not receive official recognition until 1895, by 2020 over half of all United Kingdom dentists will be women.

WORD STATION
apprentice person who learns a trade or profession by working an agreed period of time for someone who is fully trained. The apprentice usually works for low or no wages or just for food and accommodation.

At last, Dr Blackwell

When women first attempted to qualify as doctors, the biggest obstacle in their path was getting accepted for a university degree place. It did not become formally accepted that women could study at British universities until 1876, and most universitities still did not grant degrees to women who completed their courses satisfactorily. This was the problem that faced American teacher Elizabeth Blackwell (1821–1910) when she decided to train as a doctor.

The British-born 26-year-old was rejected by 29 medical schools before starting at the Geneva Medical School in New York, USA. She graduated top of her year in 1849. Blackwell went on to receive further training in Paris and London, before setting up the New York Infirmary for Women and Children in 1857. She worked in hospitals and as a medical educator for the rest of her life, inspiring young women to believe there was a place for them in medicine.

WOMEN DOCTORS

In 1851, there were no women doctors in the United Kingdom. By 1871, there were just eight. By 1901, this figure had jumped to 212.

Male students boycotted lectures and staff refused to teach her when Elizabeth Blackwell started her training.

By setting up medical schools and hospitals, such as this one pictured in the 1920s, British nurse turned doctor Elizabeth Garrett Anderson made sure women could get medical training.

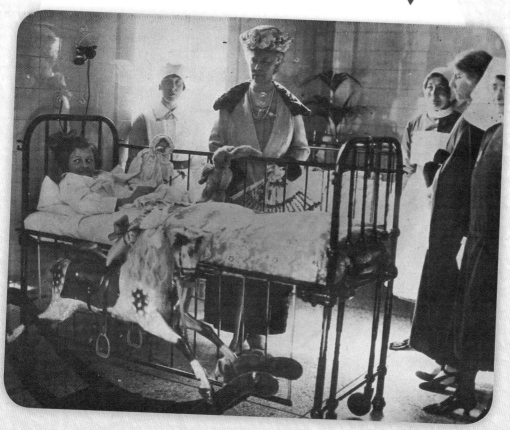

From nurse to doctor

One of those inspired to become a doctor by Elizabeth Blackwell was British nurse Elizabeth Garrett Anderson (1836–1917). For four years she applied to every college and hospital in England to study medicine, but was rejected by them all. She then followed a course of private study and was finally accepted as a doctor by the **Society of Apothecaries** in 1865.

Anderson developed a large medical practice and set up several teaching hospitals that trained women, later employing Elizabeth Blackwell as one of her lecturers.

WORD STATION
Society of Apothecaries body for pharmacists founded in 1617 and granted the right from 1815 to conduct examinations in medicine and license doctors in Britain.

37

The brain, the mind, and medicine

At the beginning of the industrial age, knowledge of the workings of the brain was limited, and attitudes towards mental illness and psychological conditions were influenced by superstition and religion. By the end of the 19th century, the science of **neurobiology** was well established and terms such as **psychiatry**, **psychology**, and **psychoanalysis** were familiar to specialists.

Mapping the brain

During the 19th century, great steps forward were taken in understanding and mapping the brain. Experiments on animals and observations of patients with injuries to specific parts of the brain made it clear that different bits of the brain were involved in different body functions. As early as 1811, Scottish surgeon Charles Bell worked out that nerves for the various senses could be traced from the sense organs to specific parts of the brain. In 1862, French neuroscientist Paul Broca located the position in the brain of the speech centre. By 1874, German Carl Wernicke's study of stroke victims and their problems mapped out the brain even further.

Although care of the mentally ill was still quite basic in the late 19th century, in most countries patients were no longer chained, starved, and filthy. This picture was taken in 1900, at the Boston Insane Hospital in the United States.

WORD STATION
psychoanalysis theory of how to treat mental disorders, focusing on the conscious mind (what someone knows she or he is thinking) and the unconscious mind (what someone does not know she or he is thinking)

Sigmund Freud argued that the mind contains both conscious and unconscious levels, and that feelings and thoughts can be hidden in the unconscious only to surface in a patient's dreams. He analysed these dreams in order to uncover his patient's true desires. His theories were often controversial but they influenced thinkers throughout the 20th century and in many fields beyond psychology.

A MEDICAL MARVEL

The story of Phineas Gage (1823–1860) revealed a lot about the workings of the brain. Gage was an American railway construction foreman who was injured in an 1848 dynamite explosion. The blast thrust a long metal bar through one side of his skull and out the other. Gage survived and quickly regained his physical and intellectual abilities. However, after the accident, his personality completely changed. He was subject to violent episodes, mood swings, and excessive swearing. Gage's injuries and the effects they had on him helped pinpoint the part of the brain – the frontal lobe – that controls personality traits and social **inhibitions**.

It's all in the mind

The renowned American doctor Benjamin Rush (1746–1813) identified various psychiatric illnesses, including addiction, as early as 1812. However, it was not until the late 1800s that German doctors such as Wilhelm Wundt and Emil Kraepelin started to research and classify mental disorders. Schizophrenia (a breakdown in logical thinking) and bipolar disorder (a form of depression) were first described at this time.

By the 1880s, Jean Marie Charcot (1825–1893), and later his famous pupil Sigmund Freud (1856–1939), developed the theories and treatments that became known as psychoanalysis. By 1900, the science of the mind was expanding in many directions.

The medical revolution

The years from the beginning of the industrial age to the dawning of the 20th century are often called the "medical revolution". However, the revolution did not happen by chance. A number of conditions developed and factors coincided that created the perfect circumstances for medicine to make huge advances.

Out with the old...

The most important thing that happened during this period was the triumph of germ theory over the idea of **contagious** disease spreading through **miasma**. Once this was understood and accepted by a majority of the medical profession, it was possible to try to prevent the spread of diseases and to develop treatments.

MEDICINE AROUND THE WORLD

By 1900, medical advances in the industrialized countries of the world had largely passed by those places that remained less developed. The continuing colonial rule by Western nations of much of the non-industrialized world brought some new ideas and treatments to these places. However, these practices were often available only to the rich and powerful. Christian medical missionaries were more likely to help the poor, but they expected people to convert to Christianity in return for treatment.

Infant mortality in the United Kingdom

During the 50 years between 1850 and 1900, the infant mortality rate in the United Kingdom dropped by half. This was one of the great achievements of the "medical revolution".

Year	deaths per 1000 live births
1850	216.8
1860	181.3
1870	175.5
1880	214.8
1890	150.7
1900	110.8

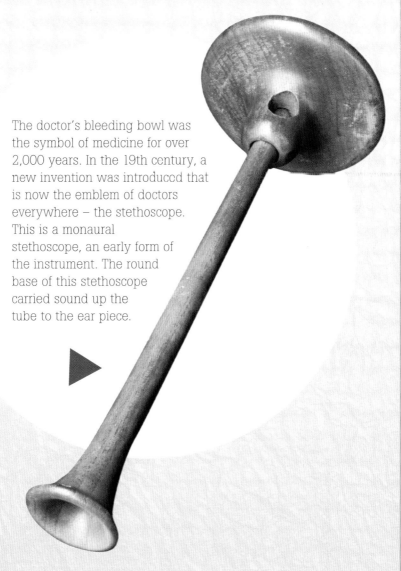

The doctor's bleeding bowl was the symbol of medicine for over 2,000 years. In the 19th century, a new invention was introduced that is now the emblem of doctors everywhere – the stethoscope. This is a monaural stethoscope, an early form of the instrument. The round base of this stethoscope carried sound up the tube to the ear piece.

In with the new

The new **antiseptics**, starting with carbolic acid, gave the medical profession one of the most important tools they needed to halt the existing massive infection rates and to make surgery safer. Pain was finally conquered by **anaesthetics**, and hospitals were no longer places of fear and death. Politicians, doctors, and engineers worked together to improve living conditions in cities. Doctors and nurses became members of well-regulated and respected professions.

However, the greatest contribution to the medical revolution came from the ideas, inventions, innovations, and discoveries of exceptional and gifted individuals. Their insights, determination, and hard work benefited everyone.

RENÉ LAËNNEC
(1781–1826)

René Laënnec was a French doctor who is remembered for having invented the monaural (one ear) stethoscope in 1816. He came up with the simple idea when he was having trouble listening to the chest of a very fat female patient with a heart condition! His first design was a plain wooden tube. Later he made one in three pieces that could be taken apart. In 1851, a binaural (two ear) stethoscope was developed by Arthur Leared, which is almost the same as the one used today.

Did you know?
Laënnec referred to the stethoscope as the "greatest legacy of my life".

Timeline

1745	The Company of Surgeons, later the Royal College of Surgeons, is founded after its separation from the Company of Barbers
1796	English doctor Edward Jenner introduces his **vaccination** against **smallpox**
1797	First government hospital in Australia at Sydney
1880–1890	Life of Edwin Chadwick, British lawyer and politician who campaigned for public health and sanitation
1816	Stethoscope invented by René Laënnec
1818-1865	Life of Ignaz Semmelweis, the Hungarian doctor who discovered that doctors were spreading diseases
1824-1834	New medical schools are founded at 12 British universities
1828	Body-snatchers Burke and Hare are arrested for murdering people to provide bodies for medical **dissection**
1832	First great cholera **epidemics** occur in the United Kingdom and the United States
1832	Provincial Medical and Surgical Association (PMSA) founded by Charles Hastings
1843-1910	Life of German medical researcher Robert Koch, who developed and proved the germ theory of disease
1845	American dentist Horace Wells first uses ether as an **anaesthetic** to relieve pain
1846	Anaesthetics are first used in surgery
1847	Chloroform is used in childbirth as an anaesthetic
1848	First British Public Health Act
1853	Hypodermic syringe is invented in France by C. G. Pravaz. It uses the hollow needle developed by Francis Rynd in 1844 to inject liquids directly into a vein.
1853–1856	Crimean War
1854	John Snow in London works out that water is responsible for the spread of cholera, not a **miasma** of disease in the air

1855	Florence Nightingale starts to improve British nursing and military conditions
1856	The PMSA becomes the British Medical Association (BMA)
1858	The Medical Act is passed in Britain establishing the General Medical Council and setting standards for medical training and professional regulation
1861–1865	American Civil War
1862	First medical school in Australia is founded at Melbourne
1865	Carbolic acid is first used as an **antiseptic** in surgery
1870	Joseph Lister's antiseptic spray is widely used in operations from this time
1870–1871	Franco-Prussian War
1873	Elizabeth Garrett Anderson is the first female member of the BMA
1874	London School of Medicine for Women is founded by Sophia Jex-Blake
1875	National Anti-Vivisection Society (NAVS) is founded in London to fight against animals being used in scientific experiments
Late 1870s	Germ theory as developed by Pasteur and Koch becomes widely accepted by scientists and medical professionals
1885	Louis Pasteur develops **rabies** immunization
1887	Hermann Biggs and T. Mitchell Prudden identify the cholera bacteria
1892	Bacteriological Laboratory of New York City is established under the leadership of Hermann Biggs, the first municipal lab in the world set up to **diagnose** diseases
1895	Aspirin is first produced by the German company Bayer
1895	Austrian psychiatrist Sigmund Freud publishes first work on **psychoanalysis**
1895	Wilhelm Roentgen makes the famous first X-ray of his wife's hand
1897	Ronald Ross proves that malaria is carried by the anopheles mosquito

Glossary

anaesthetic substance used in operations to stop a patient feeling pain

anatomy science of the structure of the human body

antiseptic prevents infection or contamination from germs and microbes

apprentice person who learns a trade or profession by working an agreed period of time for someone who is fully trained

clinical based on observation and treatment of patients

contagious able to be caught or passed from one person to another

contamination impurity from contact with something dirty or infected

corrupt dishonest

dehydration condition caused by not having enough water in the body

delouse clean someone of body and head lice

diagnose identify the nature of a disease or injury through examination

dissect cut up a dead body in order to examine it

dysentery serious infectious intestinal disease that causes violent bloody diarrhoea

dyslexic having a disorder involving difficulty in learning to read and write or interpret words and letters

epidemic rapid spread of a disease through an area or population

fermentation chemical change brought about by addition of a fermenting agent, such as yeast

hypothesis theory or unproven idea

inhibition suppression of certain behaviours or impulses that could be considered inappropriate

inoculation another term for vaccination

lesion pus-filled scab or sore, also known as a "pox"

logistical relating to the provision of facilities, movement of people, and obtaining of supplies

malnutrition condition caused by not having enough wholesome, nutritional food

miasma unpleasant or unhealthy substance in the air

microbe very tiny living thing that can carry disease

mortality death

neurobiology branch of biology that deals with the nervous system

opiate drug containing opium or made from opium

pathogen bacterium, virus, or other microbe that can cause disease

philanthropic characterized by concern for others

post-mortem examination of a body to find out about the cause of death

psychiatry branch of medicine that deals with the diagnosis and treatment of mental disorders

psychoanalysis theory of how to treat mental disorders, focusing on the conscious mind (what someone knows she or he is thinking) and the unconscious mind (what someone does not know she or he is thinking)

psychology science of the mind, mental states, and mental processes

quack unqualified person who claims to have medical knowledge

rabies disease of the nervous system caused by germs transferred in the bite of an infected animal

Society of Apothecaries body for pharmacists founded in 1617 and granted the right from 1815 to conduct examinations in medicine and license doctors in Britain

smallpox disease characterized by pus-filled blisters

statistical using numerical data to arrive at a conclusion

sterile free of bacteria

sterilize make free of bacteria

systematic doing something in an ordered, organized, and consistent way

triage assigning priority by urgency to wounds or illnesses in order to treat a large number of patients

urbanization growth of cities and towns

vaccination introducing a preparation (called a vaccine) into the body to create antibodies so the vaccinated person becomes immune and does not catch a disease

Find out more

Books

From Cowpox to Antibiotics, Carol Ballard (Raintree, 2007)

From Fail to Win! Learning from Bad Ideas: Medicine, Rebecca Vickers (Raintree, 2011)

Life and World of Florence Nightingale, Struan Reid (Heinemann Library, 2004)

Sci-Hi Scientists: The Scientists Behind Medical Advances, Eve Hartman and Wendy Meshbesher (Raintree, 2011)

Websites

www.bbc.co.uk/schools/gcsebitesize/history/shp/modern
This website covers the important events in the history of medicine during the 19th century, including information about Edward Jenner and the development of vaccination.

www.historylearningsite.co.uk/history_of_medicine.htm
Read here about many of the great medical figures of the 18th and 19th century, including Louis Pasteur and Robert Koch.

www.johnsnowsociety.org/johnsnow/facts.html
This site will give you a wealth of information about Dr John Snow and his work to trace the source of cholera epidemics.

Places to visit

Edward Jenner's House, Gloucestershire
www.jennermuseum.com

The Army Medical Services Museum, Surrey
www.ams-museum.org.uk

The Florence Nightingale Museum, London
www.florence-nightingale.co.uk

More topics to research

Learn more about discoveries, technical advances, and events:

- improved microscope lenses
- improvements in sewage treatment and water supplies
- the X-ray
- chemical engineering and the growth of the pharmaceutical industry
- medical and nursing schools
- government involvement in public health
- the development of aspirin

Learn more about people who made a difference:

- Leroy d'Etoiles and cancer statistics
- John White, surgeon of the Australian First Fleet
- James Parkinson and the disease named after him
- Early women doctors, such as Emily Blackwell, Sophia Jex-Blake, and Sarah Stephenson
- Johann Peter Frank's early public health and preventative medicine research
- The Earl of Shaftsbury's work to improve urban health and living conditions
- James Paget and medical training in the United Kingdom
- 19th century medical missionaries to Africa and Asia, such as David Livingstone
- Ronald Ross and understanding malaria
- The cover of this book shows a detail from a painting of Florence Nightingale attending a patient at Scutari Barracks, Turkey. Find out more about how Nightingale changed the study and practice of nursing once she returned to England.

Index